A Way Into Hebrews

Joy Tetley

Principal, East Anglia Ministerial Training Course

GROVE BOOKS LIMITED
RIDLEY HALL RD CAMBRIDGE CB3 9HU

Contents

1. Introduction: The Way of Life 3
2. A Community Losing Its Way 4
3. The Way of God 7
4. The New and Living Way 11
5. The Way of Christian Discipleship 16
6. The Way of Christian Leadership 20
Bibliography 23

The Cover Illustration is by Peter Ashton

Copyright © Joy Tetley 1998

First Impression June 1998
ISSN 1365-490X
ISBN 1 85174 376 6

1
Introduction: The Way of Life

Hebrews is one of the most exciting and radical books in the New Testament. It pulsates with God's transforming power. It is a work of urgent pastoral theology, confronting us with a God who is both inviting and challenging. Its anonymous author is clearly a skilled preacher, fired with pastoral passion. Its startling theology is produced not from an ivory tower but out of experience and commitment, and under the provoking pressure of crisis.

That assessment would not evoke a universally immediate 'amen'! Despite the fact that Hebrews has had a significant and permeative influence on liturgy and hymnody—and, through its 'purple passages' at least, on Christian devotion and preaching—the Epistle strikes many as 'alien' and 'difficult.' Indeed, there are those who agree with one Hebrews' scholar that we should accept the work's 'contemporary irrelevance.'[1] The impression is that the letter does not address the way we live now. Its language and thought-forms are too complex and remote for people who are no longer in touch with the cultic and ritual concerns of first century Judaism. Ironically (in view of the fact that at least one of the Epistle's main themes is direct access to God), many feel the work is distinctly inaccessible.

It would be misleading to suggest that Hebrews is an easy or straightforward read. Even its author realized that the Epistle's message was going to take some digesting (see 5.11)! Yet that message is far from irrelevant to people of another age and culture. It takes us into the depths of God and points to the fundamentals of Christian discipleship. To purloin some of his own language, the writer of Hebrews 'being dead...still speaks.'

What he says connects with not a few of the root questions of human experience and searching. If God exists, what kind of God? What is God's attitude towards humankind, and creation more generally? Does God care? Does God understand? Where is God when it comes to suffering and death? Can we trust God? Or is God more to be feared than loved? Does God speak with forked tongue—reassuring us with one voice and demanding impossible standards with the other? Does God truly love us?

All these questions (and more!) are highlighted by a serious engagement with Hebrews. Its language might need some translating but its message has lost none of its power. Searching for God in Hebrews (even as we approach a new millennium) can still change lives for good.

My prayer is that what follows in this booklet, though at best it can only skim the surface, might stir up some desire to delve deeper into a work that is alive with the living God.

---

[1] R Williamson, 'Hebrews and Doctrine,' *Expository Times* Vol 81, 1969-70.

2
A Community Losing Its Way

The people addressed by Hebrews were clearly a community in crisis. The text suggests that they were disheartened, confused, afraid and ready to give up. They were facing hostility which was so severe that it was undermining their commitment to Jesus. It seems likely that they were Jewish Christians who, under the threat of persecution, felt strongly drawn back to a Judaism which did not acknowledge Jesus.[2] Certainly they were Christians of some years standing who in the early years of their faith had successfully faced challenging opposition (10.32–34). By the time Hebrews was written, however, their confidence was all but gone. Traditionally, this community has been sited in Rome at a time when Christians were subjected to the emperor's disfavour (during the reign of Nero in the 60s AD, for example). Other scholarly suggestions include Alexandria and Corinth.[3]

The Author
The author was evidently someone who knew this community well; someone who had authority over them but who, for some reason, could not be with them in person. He (or, just possibly, she)[4] did not write them a letter, so much as a 'word of exhortation' (13.22). In effect, the writer has sent them a sermon, which would have been read out when they were assembled for worship. It is a sermon born of the preacher's urgent concern, at this critical time, to keep them on the way of Jesus. They had need of endurance and of bold faith. In urging them to keep going (together, not just as individuals), the preacher seeks to communicate fresh hope by opening up a renewed vision of God in Jesus. Alongside that vision, and arising out of the preacher's acute sense of the severity of the crisis, is an impressionistic picture of the dire consequences of apostasy, of turning against Jesus.

This preacher is on fire with God and with pastoral zeal. Yet his passion is expressed through a work that is carefully structured and carefully argued. Both mind and heart are very much engaged. God and God's mission of salvation constitute the primary focus. The language and imagery used have much to do with worship and means of access to God. And in all this, Jesus is crucial. For the writer of Hebrews, 'looking to Jesus' (12.2) means seeing into the life and character of God (1.1–3; 2.9,14).

Hebrews is pastoral theology forged out of dynamic, experiential faith. Its author was clearly well educated, both in terms of matters Jewish and of Greek rhetoric. He knew how to put an argument together and express it effectively—

---

[2] See H W Attridge, *Hebrews* (London: Hermeneia, 1989) pp 9–13.
[3] See P Ellingworth, *Hebrews* (Grand Rapids: Eerdmans, 1993) pp 28–29.
[4] A Harnack many years ago suggested that the writer was Priscilla.

witness, for example, his use of alliteration and metaphor, his capacity to communicate heights and depths, encouragement and fear; to touch the feelings as well as search the mind. He is, at the same time, theological poet, committed pastor, acute thinker, powerful preacher, verbal strategist, spiritual visionary and, above all, devoted lover of the God of Jesus Christ.

Though 'Hebrews as rhetoric' is currently one of the main emphases of Hebrew scholarship,[5] no-one has yet been able to fit the work precisely into a particular rhetorical form. The writer of Hebrews is his own person. He is not a slave to 'correct structure' but a servant of God. He draws on all his skills, not to make an impression for the sake of it, not to make a name for himself, but to persuade a community in spiritual danger to hold on, to look to Jesus, to keep on choosing life.

Hebrews' Use of the Old Testament

For the writer of Hebrews (who surely had a Jewish background)[6] the Jewish Scriptures were, without doubt, the word of God. Time and again, the quotations he uses are said to be spoken by God,[7] the Holy Spirit[8] or Jesus.[9] This does not mean that he regarded human agency as unimportant. Divine and human contributions are brought together interestingly at 3.7 and 4.7, where Psalm 95.7 is attributed first to the Holy Spirit and then to David. Human beings need to hear and respond to God's voice (a major Hebrews theme) but it is God who speaks (see 1.1–2).

Hebrews' motivating belief in Jesus as the Christ, the Son of God, provides the hermeneutical framework within which interpretation of Jewish Scriptures is undertaken. So it is that the catena of texts used in 1.5–13 are taken as spoken by God to or of the Son. And to bring out something of the significance of Christ and his vocation, a number of Scriptures are put onto the lips of Jesus (Psalm 22.22 and Isaiah 8.17–18 at Heb 2.12–13; Psalm 40.6–8 at Heb 10.5–10).

Throughout, Hebrews uses Greek versions of Jewish texts (and not always the Septuagint as we know it). It would not be at all surprising if there were Greek texts available at this time of which we have no knowledge. It may also be the case, of course, that the writer of Hebrews was working from memory. Certainly he seems to have no qualms about changing the wording of a quotation within a short compass in his own sermon (compare his citation of Jeremiah 31.31f at Heb 8.8–12 and 10.16–17). For Hebrews it was not the precise form of words that mattered but the substance of what God was saying.

As will be indicated later, Hebrews' understanding of God is decidedly Deuteronomic. It is also the case that in reflecting on the provisions for approaching

---

5 See D F Watson, 'Rhetorical Criticism of Hebrews and the Catholic Epistles' in *Currents in Research: Biblical Studies* (Sheffield Academic Press, 1997) pp 175–207.
6 See Ellingworth (1993) pp 3–21.
7 1.5–13; 5.5–6; 6.13–14; 7.21; 8.8–13; 10.30; 12.25–26; 13.5.
8 3.7–11; 10.15–17.
9 2.12–13; 10.5–10.

God in the Jewish tradition, he concentrates his attention on liturgical arrangements as set out in the Pentateuch. It is the worship of Tabernacle rather than Temple that Hebrews uses by way of illustration, comparison and contrast. Theologically, this fits well with his concern that the new covenant people of God should be a people on the move, a people who have no 'abiding city,' a people travelling to their promised rest with God. It also enables him to emphasize how Jesus, the 'pioneer' leader far greater than Moses, brings to their true fulfilment, their 'end,' all the careful provisions made to enable sinful human beings to have safe communion with the living God.

3
The Way of God

To the composer of Hebrews God meant everything. His 'word of exhortation' is thoroughly theocentric. God is the dominant subject throughout. Often that is the case grammatically. It is no accident, for example, that the opening sentence (1.1–4) and the closing benediction (13.20, 21)—both summary 'nutshells' which explode with significance—have God as their definitive subject. Here grammar is expressive of a far deeper reality:[10] that God is all in all; the source and energy of creation, more powerful than death, pro-active and multi-faceted in communication, always working to bring out the best, a God of intimate relationship and sacrificial grace.

This God is the driving force, the urgent inspiration behind all that Hebrews says, even when the divine name is not mentioned. The one who is Son, whom 'in the days of his flesh' we come to know as Jesus, is none other than the ultimate self-expression of God (1.2,3). When we hear what is 'spoken through the Lord' (2.3), we hear the authoritative and authentic word of God. When we 'look to Jesus' (2.9; 12.2), we see into the life and character of God. When we 'pay attention' to Jesus (3.1; 12.3), we discover the encouragement of God for our pilgrimage. And when we consider the examples (both positive and negative) of God's people of old (see, for example, 3–4; 11.4–38), we do so in the light of their relationship with the God who calls them to commitment and holiness. The God of Hebrews will not, so to speak, leave us alone. For good or ill, we cannot escape the impact of this God's presence.

Searching God

So it must have been for the writer of Hebrews. For him, God was not simply the answer to the community's crisis (though that, certainly, he believed to be the case). God was also at the heart of the crisis. God was question as well as answer. During this time of trial, there were many things to ask of God; and, still more importantly, God had much to ask of these wavering children of the new covenant—for and to whom so much had been given, at inexpressible cost. This relationship was at a crucial point—a cross-roads. Were this community to turn back or turn aside, they would be walking away from the only one who could truly and entirely meet them where they were and lead them into glory. Such rejection of the God with whom they had entered into the most intimate of covenants (see 8–10) could only bring profound and painful grief—on both sides. For God, it would (yet again) be excruciating (see 6.6). For those who have abandoned God—

---

10 So also in the Jewish Scriptures. See W Brueggemann, *Theology of the Old Testament* (Fortress, 1997) pp 408–12.

and become actively hostile in the process—the prospect is bleak indeed (10.26-31).

It must be noted, however, that the clear emphasis in Hebrews' overall presentation of God is both positive and inviting. The 'severe passages' (notably 2.1-3; 6.4-8; 10.26-31; 12.25-29) must be taken both in their immediate context and with due attention to the author's contemporary setting and purpose. These warnings do not stand alone.[11] They are part of a pastoral strategy, designed to keep a faltering community on course. That involves showing graphically how much can be lost, thereby further highlighting the inestimable blessings to be enjoyed at God's hands. It is only a fearful thing to fall into those hands (10.31) if you have treated what they offer with utter and savage contempt (10.29). As Hebrews puts it immediately after an earlier diatribe, 'Even though we speak in this way, beloved, we are confident of better things in your case...' (6.9). Here is a preacher making telling use of what we might call the 'worst-case scenario.' Yet, as Attridge points out, 'the accent in his treatment falls on the...more hopeful part of his exhortation.'[12]

It is not surprising that at times strong language is used. Hebrews was dealing with a critical situation. Apostasy seems to have been a real danger, and for the author of Hebrews, the kind of apostasy he fears amounts to nothing less than the callous betrayal of God. We should remember in this context that a horrifying act of treachery by one of Christ's chosen disciples had deepened the darkness of his passion. The 'Judas factor,' so near the centre of the gospel story, must have made apostasy seem especially abhorrent to the early Christian communities. Certainly, the language used of apostates by Hebrews is decidedly personal, and has its focus on the crucified Lord. They crucify the Son of God afresh, and hold him up to open shame (6.6). They trample on the Son of God, treat the blood of the covenant (Christ's blood) as something profane, and outrage the Spirit of grace (10.29). They have deliberately chosen to become enemies of God (10.26,27). They will have their reward (10.27,30,31).

It may also be that there is the real prospect of treachery against Christ being expressed through the betrayal (the 'handing over') of sisters and brothers in Christ. Under pressure of persecution, reneging on one's own Christian profession and informing on fellow Christians might well be seen as a way of (physical) salvation. We hear from a grudgingly sympathetic Tacitus, for example, that in Nero's Rome, after the fire, the emperor scapegoated 'a class hated for their abominations, who are commonly called Christians.'

So 'arrest was first made of those who confessed [ie to being Christians], then on their evidence an immense multitude was convicted.'[13] In Mark's Gospel (also traditionally associated with Rome), Jesus is recorded as warning that 'brother will betray brother to death...But the one who endures to the end will be saved'

---

11 Hebrews is not concerned here with what *later* became the issue of 'post-baptismal sin.'
12 Attridge, p 167.
13 Tacitus, *Annales* xv 44.

THE WAY OF GOD

(see Mark 13.9–13). Hebrews, too, lays great stress on the need for endurance—and a fair weight of tradition locates the addressees in Rome. They have not yet resisted to the point of shedding their blood. By implication that might become necessary. In any event, they must actively support, not abandon one another, remembering those in prison as though in prison with them and looking to the One who endured (through betrayal and misrepresentation) all manner of hostility, shame and suffering. He alone can lead them into the joy of salvation which is eternal.[14]

Covenant God

God will not be mocked—not, at least, by those who have freely taken advantage of God's costly blessings and then cast them in his teeth. For this is the God of the covenant. As far as the author of Hebrews is concerned, though the details of the covenant might change, the character of the covenant God does not. Deuteronomic theology seems to have particularly influenced him in this regard. The majority of those passages which underline the fearfulness of God are direct quotations from or allusions to Deuteronomy.[15] Quite evidently, whatever covenant is being talked about, God is the senior partner. Indeed, it is God who takes the initiative in establishing the relationship, motivated by a love that is fierce yet tender, and characterized by a commitment that is absolute in its faithfulness. God looks for a like response in his beloved covenanted people. Forsaking all others, they must worship God, and God alone; they must love God with all their heart, soul and strength; they must hear and obey God's voice. This 'marriage,' with all its potential for rich fruitfulness, is for life. Unfaithfulness is not an option. When God's people treat him with careless abandon, God is cut to the quick—and reacts accordingly.[16] Yet this leaves God, as it were, with a dilemma—one that is expressed with particular (often violent) power in the prophecy of Hosea, 'How can I give you up...?'[17] How can the God who loves with an everlasting love (Jeremiah 31.3) reject the beloved? How can the absolutely faithful God break faith?

As Brueggemann puts it, according to 'Israel's testimony,' there is 'an unresolve in the character of Yahweh.'[18] That is reflected in the testimony of Hebrews. What is also reflected is the Jewish tradition's primary stress on God's steadfast love, compassion and mercy. The Judaeo-Christian God, even when expressing anger, is 'passionately attentive.'[19]

This, of course, is the language, the experiential 'stuff' of personal relationship. We recognize it in our hearts. For Hebrews, this is what 'covenant' is about. The new covenant, brought into being with so much blood and suffering, offers

---

14 See Hebrews 10.23–25; 12.2–4; 13.3,12–14.
15 Heb 10.28/Deut 17.6; Heb 10.30/Deut 32.35–36; Heb 12.18ff/Deut 4.11,36; 5.23; 9.19; Heb 12.29/Deut 4.24; 9.3.
16 See, for example, Deut 6.4–15
17 Hosea 11.8–9. Compare 13.4–14.8.
18 Brueggemann, *Theology*, p 411.
19 Brueggemann, *Theology*, p 491.

an intimacy with God that is beyond all telling—yet which must be shared. It is for 'all,' without distinction. And it is first and foremost a community experience, not an individualistic indulgence (8.10–12; see also 4.12–16). It is with the whole community of faith that God has made covenant. So when some fall away or fall prey to bitterness, that community, too, feels the disintegrating, poisoning effect (see for example 10.23–26; 12.14,15).

Enterprising and Committed God
The God of Hebrews is a God who desires passionately to be 'known.' Not just known about, but known in the closest, most personal and interactive of relationships. (Such is most often the sense of the verb as used in the Scriptures. In this regard, Hebrews stands in a long tradition.) This is a God who, though 'one and only,' knows relationship within the divine being and experience; a God who in creating, sustaining, communicating and saving, works through partnership—primarily with the Son and the Spirit, but also with those people of faith who respond with obedience to the promptings of God's word (see especially 1.1–4; 2.3; 3.14). This is a God who takes initiatives 'in many and various ways,' who seizes opportunities and explores possibilities, however costly the risk. This is a God of energy, who takes the lead and shows the way. This is a faithful God who will never fail or forsake, though he be forsaken. And, clearly, this is a holy God to whom ultimate power and authority belong. God is 'judge of all' (12.23).

But God is no unjust judge (6.10). At his throne, the 'quality of mercy' is to be found in abundance, not to mention 'grace abounding' (4.16). It also matters vitally that God exemplifies what is being asked of those who sooner or later come before him: faithfulness, endurance, boldness, in-depth understanding, compassion, forgiveness. The God who yearns for us to 'know him' knows from the inside what it means to be human in a world out of joint.

Supremely, from our perspective, this God speaks decisively in one who is Son, in Jesus (1.2,3; 4.14). In so doing, God gives emphatic (not to say shocking) expression to the desire of his heart, and the character of his ministry and mission. God opens up a 'new and living way' (10.20).

4
The New and Living Way

The author of Hebrews has clearly been captivated by Jesus. He uses the name 'Jesus,' usually without qualification, over a dozen times, and (in the Greek) it invariably comes in an emphatic position at the beginning or end of a phrase. So, for example, the familiar exhortation in 12.2 reads literally 'looking away into the pioneer and perfecter of our faith, Jesus.' The overwhelming impression is that the author of Hebrews is speaking of someone he knows, someone in and through whom, he is convinced, we can meet with the living God.

Jesus the Son of God

For Hebrews, Jesus is the Son of God. To illuminate the transforming implications of this identification, the writer makes use of a range of available interpretative models, all of which when applied to Jesus turn out to be decidedly radical. From the first two chapters alone (chapters which are in effect an overture introducing the composer's main themes) we are encouraged to 'see Jesus' as (amongst other things!) God's wisdom, God's mouthpiece/prophet, God's defining, redeeming and sanctifying word, God's servant, God's true Adam, the Pioneer of salvation, the vanquisher of the devil, the liberator from enslaving fear of death, the glorious King of creation, and—focally—God's merciful and faithful High Priest. In itself, this is imagery that derives from the author's Jewish heritage or, as in the case of *archegos* / pioneer for example, from his wider cultural milieu.[20] Yet viewed in the light of his fundamental conviction as to the identity of Jesus, it all takes on a distinctly revolutionary edge. We might say that christology gives way to theology. Contemplating Jesus gives us insight into God which is at once authoritative, encouraging and disturbing.

Jesus the Wisdom of God

The opening sentence of Hebrews (1.1–4), reinforced by the rest of the majestic opening chapter, provides us with the vital key. The Son in whom God has spoken definitively to us, the Son through whom God created and sustains the world is 'the radiance/reflection[21] of God's glory and exact imprint (*charakter*) of God's very being.' At the eternal heart of God's being, it seems, is relationship and (literally) co-operation. Here, the Son is spoken of in language used by Jewish writers to describe God's Wisdom (compare especially Proverbs 8.22–31 and Wisdom of Solomon 7.24–47, where *apaugasma* is used of Wisdom). For Hellenistic Jews particularly, the figure of Wisdom (*Sophia*) had come to express in poetic form the active relationship between God and creation. Wisdom is presented as

---

[20] See W L Lane, *Hebrews* (Waco: Word, 1991) Vol 1, p 56f.
[21] *apaugasma* can mean either.

the personification of God's attitude towards and involvement with the created order. For those bound to strict monotheism, this was a metaphor both suggestive and daring. If taken too literally, Wisdom could be seen as a separate divine being—even a divine consort. Yet there is, perhaps, in this perception of *Sophia* an intuitive awareness of variety and inter-relatedness within the one God. And Wisdom is a very attractive figure, vibrant with creative life, one who conveys both delight and authority, one who opens up and shares the workings of God, one who is exalted with God.[22]

Not surprisingly, what is said about God's Wisdom comes to be seen by many early Christians as highly applicable to Jesus.[23] The 'Jesus experience' was overwhelming and comprehensive in its transforming power. In trying to express its significance, Christians began to explore Jesus' relationship with the living God and to explore it in terms of person rather than personification. For Jesus was not just a poetic perception. He had been a flesh and blood human being—a truth Hebrews is at pains to underline (see for example 2.5–18; 4.15–5.10; 10.19–22). Jesus suffered and died—in a dreadful way. Yet he produced 'God-like' effects, both before and after his physical death. What on earth (and in heaven) was to be made of him?

Jesus the Expression of God

For Hebrews, as for the other NT writers, this was no academic question. In the most profound sense, life depended on it. The strange (yet also strangely familiar) wisdom of God is fully exposed in Jesus. Jesus is none other than God's own self-expression—God's 'Son' in a far deeper and more direct sense than those of whom that ascription had formerly been used.[24] All that we see in Jesus, claims Hebrews, speaks of the very character of God. So we see a God who, rather than deploring and punishing our condition, enters into it, feeling in Jesus the full force of temptation and human frailty (2.9,10,14,17; 4.15; 5.7; 12.3; 13.12,13). In Jesus, God identifies with us. In Jesus, God draws near to where we are, inviting us to draw near with confidence to him. In Jesus, and at tremendous cost, God knows, God understands, God cares. And out of that knowing God can bring deep encouragement and mighty help (4.16).

This was something the battered Hebrews congregation (and not only they) needed to hear and receive. God had not abandoned them. God was going through these fearful trials with them. God knew what it was like to feel afraid and pushed to the limit. God was holding on to them—and urging them to hold on to him.

Jesus, Mediator of God's New Covenant

They were also being urged not to let go of the limitless blessings integral to that new covenant relationship with God inaugurated through the pain and death

---

[22] See Wisdom of Solomon 6.12–10.21.
[23] See, for example, John 1.1–11; 1 Cor 8.6; Col 1.15–19; Rev 3.14.
[24] For example, Adam, Israel, the king.

of Jesus. Forgiveness, grace, sharing the life of God—all these were there for the accepting. Throwing away such gifts would be loss indeed.

For Hebrews, this new covenant,[25] this fulfilment of prophecy,[26] was without doubt the covenant to end all covenants. Nothing more could be added or offered. It was, so to speak, 'fully comprehensive,' with everything written in 'bold' and nothing hidden in the small print. But unlike earthly insurance policies, God's new covenant is not established as a legal contract.[27] It is an invitation (at God's expense) to enter into a profound and direct relationship with God that needs no intermediaries; an intimate relationship in which, incredibly, God both forgives and forgets (10.15–17). And it is a relationship open to all, from the least to the greatest (8.11). In God's new covenant, all relate to God on the same terms. There can be no privileged groups with a special knowledge that brings them closer to God than those outside their circle. The only 'qualification' needed to know the God of Jesus Christ is to have said 'Yes' to his sacrificially loving proposal—and (like God) to stick with it through good times and bad.

Jesus is the mediator of this new covenant (9.15; 12.24). As such, his ministry is far more significant and effective than those who mediated the Sinai covenant (the angels and Moses). Jesus fulfils Jeremiah's prophecy as God's self-expression (1.1–13). That, indeed, was 'fitting.' Jeremiah's prophecy makes it clear that the establishment of the new covenant was the direct responsibility of God, a fact reflected in the number of first person singulars to be found in the Old Testament passage (nine in all). Hebrews reinforces this 'direct action' on the part of God by ascribing the prophecy to God (8.8) and the Holy Spirit (10.15)—and supremely by his bold understanding of Jesus as Son of God.

Though Moses, at least, if not the angels, went through a fair amount of suffering in obediently communicating the Sinai covenant to God's people, he did not approach the extremity of passion required of the Son of God. Jesus opened up the possibility of heart-to-heart communion between humankind and God at the cost of temptation, shame, hostility, heart-breaking anguish—and finally at the cost of his own life.

Jesus as Priest and Victim

The fact and the nature of Jesus' death was integral to early Christian experience and preaching. But how could the significance and impact of Christ's crucifixion be articulated and communicated? Attempts had to be made to express its life-changing meaning in terms that people could begin to understand from their own background and context. The New Testament gives us a considerable range of such attempts. As far as Hebrews is concerned, the author discerned and shared a vision which was both ground-breaking and boundary-crossing. It was a vision that was without precedent—relating the prophecy of a new covenant to the

---

[25] See also Mark 14.24; 1 Cor 11.25; 2 Cor 3.6.
[26] Jeremiah 31.31ff—quoted *in extenso* at Heb 8.8–12 and 10.16–17.
[27] Even in the imagery of a 'will and testament' (9.15–18) the personal dimension is uppermost.

purpose and ritual of the Jewish Day of Atonement, and ascribing the complete fulfilment of both to one who, as self-expression of God and great High Priest, offered, once for all, the fully efficacious sacrifice of himself. Even for a community that shared the writer's background and milieu, that was, in the jargon of a later age, 'mind-blowing.'

What might have influenced and clarified this vision for the writer of Hebrews has for long been a lively subject of debate. Clearly his own religious and cultural heritage (and probably that of his community) have provided him with much of his language and imagery, his means of articulation.[28] Urgent impetus has also come from the parlous spiritual state of those addressed. But the crucial dimension, surely, springs out of his own experience, through the ever living Jesus, of direct access to the 'throne of grace;' of personal, liberating, grace-filled communion with God.

Such was the promise of the new covenant. Such, too, was the goal of priesthood. Both involved tackling the great barrier of sin; of that which poisons human living and relationships, warps creation and stands in the way of full communion with the absolutely holy God. Through Jeremiah's prophecy God says, 'I will remember their sins no more' (31.34). Hebrews is keenly aware that this was no casual statement on the part of God. Sin is a serious business. And so is the determined love of God. To make plain the enormity of what God had to go through in order to bring that home to us, Hebrews turns to what is familiar—to Jewish understandings of priesthood and sacrifice. In doing so (explicitly and at length) he is unique among NT writers.

Hebrews 'sees Jesus' as the integrated fulfilment, the 'end' of the priestly/sacrificial system. That system, Hebrews has no doubt, was given by God. But human frailty and fallenness could not fully realize its intended potential. It remained but a shadow of what it could be. And its provision had to be repeated, year after year (see 10.1–3; 10.11).

That was focally true of the Day of Atonement ritual (see Leviticus 16) to which Hebrews gives considerable attention. On this Day, the High Priest (and he alone) went into the Holy of Holies, the innermost sanctuary where God was believed specially to dwell. On behalf of all the people he offered the blood of animal sacrifice, praying that by this offering, with the repentance it betokened, God would set aside the people's sins. But no high priest, despite all the purification rites he went through, could presume to claim that he brought back to the people full and final assurance of God's forgiveness.

Except Jesus: our great High Priest, and Son of God. He indeed has 'once for all...put away sin by the sacrifice of himself' (9.26). This Jesus is both priest and victim. And this Jesus, despite the most extreme provocations, remained totally faithful to God and God's way. Even through 'loud cries and tears' (5.7) Jesus was obedient. His life, 'without blemish' (9.14) but certainly not without struggle, constituted the perfect offering: life given over totally to God; life poured out on

---

[28] See Attridge, pp 97–103.

behalf of all others, the ultimate expression of vicarious repentance and pure love. He did what no-one else could do, in order that everyone might know forgiveness and enjoy life with God. Through the tearing apart of the 'curtain' of his flesh (10.20) the way is opened for all to enter the Holy of Holies. Having done his unique work of bringing God and humankind together for good (the essence of priesthood), this high priest in no sense reserves the most sacred space for himself. All are welcome at the very throne of grace. From God's perspective, that is the point of it all.

In the light of God's astounding behaviour in Jesus, it must come as no surprise that in doing his priestly work, God does not fit in with existing traditions and expectations (even those which originated from divine 'decree'!). This is something of what is meant by priesthood 'after the order of Melchizedek.'[29] Melchizedek was a mysterious priest, greatly honoured by God, but not a member of the tribe of Levi nor even of the chosen race. He was an unqualified outsider who played an extremely marginal part in the history of the people of God (mentioned only in Gen 14 and Ps 110.4). Using a technical form of argument common in Judaism, Hebrews concludes that the outsider Melchizedek, king and priest, was greater than Abraham and Levi. His priesthood was of a different and superior order (7.1–10). In this (and in his messianic qualities of righteousness and peace) Melchizedek resembles the priestly Son of God. Jesus is, of course, far greater than Melchizedek, but it is this strange king's sort of priesthood that Jesus expresses to perfection—and for ever.

Jesus did not come from the right tribe to be a priest (7.13–14)—and Jesus died in disgrace 'outside the camp' (13.13). When bringing the blessings of salvation, God does a shockingly new thing. Such 'a change in the law' (7.12) is not always easy to come to terms with. Nor is the God who will not be bound by tradition—or by anything else, except steadfast love (6.13–20). Yet however unsettling it is, we must open ourselves to this God. For, as L S Thornton put it many years ago, 'the priesthood of Christ is the priesthood of God incarnate.'[30]

In a nutshell—and to use phraseology that is intriguingly popular in our 'post-Christian' society—what Hebrews is claiming is that in Jesus, God 'goes to hell and back,' for us and with us. And whatever our earthly circumstances, heaven is ours for the entering.

---

29 In the NT, only Hebrews uses v 4 of Psalm 110 as well as v 1. On Melchizedek, see Attridge, pp 192–195.
30 L S Thornton, *Doctrine of the Atonement* (London, 1937) p 107.

5
The Way of Christian Discipleship

Hebrews most certainly sends a vital message to the people of God, both then and now. It is striking how, throughout the Epistle, the people are in much stronger focus than their leaders. Whatever the influence of contextual particularities in this regard, such a focus is closely associated with the author's theological understanding.

New Covenant Privileges and Responsibilities

It is the Christian laos of God who are addressed directly by the preacher of Hebrews. He sees them as being in real continuity with the covenant people of God through all generations. From God's people of old, they can learn both what to avoid like the plague (disobedience and lack of endurance) and what to imitate with all their strength (perseverance and steadfast faith, even in situations of extreme testing; the willingness to move forward as pilgrims). And Hebrews is in no doubt that the new covenant people of God bear the prime responsibility for their own pilgrimage. They are directly accountable to God. They must make their own decisions. They must take on the consequences of their faith (or lack of it). Whatever leaders are for, they are not there to lead people's lives for them. This theme of the responsibility (and privilege) of the people of God permeates the whole of Hebrews' sermon.

It flows from the people's status as beneficiaries of the new covenant. As such they have been taken into intimate relationship with God. They are God's children; brothers and sisters of Jesus (2.10ff), members of God's household (3.5–6; 10.21). They are a worshipping community (12.22–24, 28) looking to Jesus, the very self-expression of God (1.1–4; 12.2), who is both ahead of them (2.10) and right in the middle of them (2.12). Jesus joins in their worship and teaches them of God (2.12,13). Through Jesus, they all have direct and confident access to the presence of God (4.16; 10.19–22). They need no intermediaries. They still have sacrifices to offer, but now they are sacrifices of praise and generosity (13.15–16), the surrender to God of a life of dedicated faithfulness (10.19–39; 12.14–29).

They are to listen for God's voice in the present ('today,' as Hebrews is fond of saying, 3.12–4:11), for they are living in the end-time before the final coming of God (1.2; 9.28). This means paying close attention to Jesus (3.1), in whose life they are called to share (3.4). So they must be a pilgrim people, characterized by steadfast endurance and a willingness to leave the past behind. They are moving towards God's rest, their rich reward (10.35, 36). Yet paradoxically, they can already experience it through prayer and worship (4.16; 10.19–22; 12.22–24).

With all this they should be a growing and maturing people, developing the capacity to teach the things of God (5.11–6.2). They should hold together as God's family (10.25), encouraging and exhorting one another to love, good works and steadfast faith, taking responsibility for one another's spiritual welfare (12.15). Together they must be prepared for hard struggle, abuse and suffering, seeing this as part of their training to be like Jesus (12.3–4). Through their commitment, and the working of God within them (13.21), they will discover eternal joy; they will come into their own; they will share the life and ministry of the God who created them for glory, working in partnership with God to care for creation and draw out its best potential (2.5–10). They could not wish for a more fulfilling destiny. But they are free to throw it all away.

Going 'Outside the Camp'
If the people of God are to maintain their strength and confidence through thick and thin, urges Hebrews, they must indeed look to Jesus—and make in his direction. But where is that? Heaven certainly; but there is another, distinctly earthly dimension. Movement towards Jesus will not always seem like a heavenly experience. 'The bodies of those animals whose blood is brought into the sanctuary by the high priest as a sacrifice for sin are burned outside the camp,' the preacher reminds his Jewish Christian congregation. 'Therefore Jesus also suffered outside the gate in order to sanctify the people through his own blood.' Here is contextual theology. But like all true theology, it has searching consequences for all human life. The preacher continues: 'Let us then go to him outside the camp and bear the abuse he endured' (13.10–13). 'Outside the camp'—the place for those who were polluted and defiled, the place for things of no further use, the place where rubbish was dumped and criminals executed. Looking to Jesus, following Jesus, means that earthly security and respectability have to be abandoned as priorities. For Christ's sake, Christ's followers have to be prepared to be treated as rubbish—and worse! For Christ's sake, Christ's followers may well have to be 'countercultural'—and pay the price. For those culturally schooled to prize 'honour' and to regard 'shame' as a mortal wound, that price would be high indeed. Yet at the same time, they are called to offer up continually a sacrifice of praise to God. Praise from the refuse tip; praise from a locus of uncleanness, marginalization, rejection, uselessness and contempt; praise from a place of danger, exclusion, shame and loneliness.

What is this strange praise, this costly sacrifice? 'The fruit of lips that confess God's name.' Faithfulness. Obedient discipleship. Persevering worship. Speaking out boldly for God. All this, not just occasionally but continually. Not to satisfy God's vanity or to twist God's arm, but to identify with God in his mission of love; to respond with the will if not with the feelings to the extremity of God's grace; to become party to the opening up of opportunities for God.

For the truth is that, in the strange mercy of God, the 'unholy place' becomes the Holy of Holies. The tent of meeting is again pitched 'outside the camp' (Exodus 33.7–11) but in a way that requires a radical shift in understanding. We meet with God where we least expect him. And we may well be called to suffer with him there.

Prayer-partners

'Pray for us...' urges the writer of Hebrews (13.18). As one clearly in some kind of leadership role, he recognized his need of the people's prayers—and had no hesitation in asking for them. In fact his request, far from being apologetic, verges on the directive! He was convinced, it seems, that the prayers of God's people could be powerfully effective, even when they themselves were in a debilitating state of disillusionment and confusion.

What is more, he not only asks for prayer for himself and, perhaps, for his associates (note the interesting change of pronoun between 13.18 and 13.19); he also exhorts his listeners to something we might describe as 'incarnational praying.' A striking example of this is to be found at 13.4: 'Remember those who are in prison as though you were in prison with them; those who are being tortured, as though you yourselves were being tortured.' For Hebrews, remembering in prayer involves far more than a brief recollection. It calls for a demanding empathy, an identification with those being prayed for. It means, in some strong sense, entering into their situation, even as it is held at the throne of grace; feeling something of their experience, even as it is offered into the life of God.

That is a very tall order. Still more so, when we recall the condition of that Hebrews congregation. They were hardly at the peak of spiritual fitness and commitment. And the grim circumstances they were being urged to make an imaginative reality in their prayers (imprisonment, torture) were the very horrors from which (quite understandably) they in their own context were trying to run away. Such incarnational praying for others would force them to confront their own fears.

But this kind of prayer is thoroughly consistent with the whole tenor of the Hebrews' sermon. Through his experience of Jesus, the preacher believes without reserve in a God of incarnation. It is this God who is the source and epitome of intercession. The prayer of this God is ceaseless. Prayer was evidently present in the earthly life of Jesus. It is the profound and transforming perception of Hebrews that it is also a continuing feature of what we might call the priestly ministry of Jesus in heaven. 'Consequently,' says the preacher at 7.25, Jesus 'is able to save for all time those who approach God through him, since he always lives to make intercession for them.'

This does not mean that Jesus is pleading with God to help us. Even less does it mean that Jesus is seeking to persuade God to have mercy on us. We need to remember (and in the strong Hebrews sense of that verb) that, according to this preacher, Jesus is the self-expression of God. The priesthood of Jesus is the fleshing out of God's own priestly character—God's determined yearning that all should know him, all should share his life. The mission of Jesus is the mission of God. The offering of Jesus is the offering of God. And that offering is 'once for all,' a truth heavily underlined by the preacher of Hebrews. What God has done in and through Jesus is eternally and entirely effective. God needs no persuading. If God had not been fundamentally for us, the mission of Jesus would never have happened. It was a mission which showed once and for all that God is essentially and actively gracious. God did not turn away from us in wrathful disgust, nor did God turn towards us in destructive judgment. God came to us, in great humility, meeting us on our own ground. If there is any pleading to be done, it is, rather, God pleading with us to respond to his love, to accept and take into our lives the benefits of his costly offering. God's sacrifice is complete. What more could we do to open his heart?

What, then, is this 'intercession for us' in which Jesus is continually engaged? The Greek verb used at this point is an interesting one and may give us something of a clue. In the secular usage of the time, it carries the sense of turning to and meeting with someone. That meeting might well be on behalf of others; to advance their cause or, conversely, to undermine their position. Here in Hebrews, the process is utterly positive. Jesus takes our humanity with him into the life of God—our precious, brittle humanity, with all its potential for glory and for shame. As God in Jesus met with us where we are, so Jesus in God becomes a redeeming, transfiguring meeting-place between God-ness and human-ness. This is the perfection of priestly ministry. The intercession of Jesus, our great high priest, is none other than the holding of us, constantly, at the loving, knowing heart of God.

And as the people of God draw near to the throne of grace, they are invited to identify with this divine intercession; to become, effectively, prayer-partners of God.

6
The Way of Christian Leadership

If the people of God have such a comprehensive vocation and responsibility, what place is left for leaders?

Three times in chapter 13, Hebrews highlights the community's leaders (vv 7, 17, 24). Interestingly, these are the only occasions in the whole Epistle where leaders are specifically mentioned. Even then, the preacher does not address them directly (contrast, for example 1 Timothy 6.11–21; 1 Peter 5.1–4). In fact, at v 24, the people are exhorted to greet their leaders on behalf of the preacher. That raises the question as to whether their leaders are even present at their gathering. If not, why was this assembly taking place without them? Has there been some kind of breakdown in relationships? Or are the leaders, though contactable, prevented by their circumstances from being present (in detention, perhaps, because of hostile secular authorities?) Are the addressees a disaffected house group among a network of Christian groups in the city where they are located? Like so much to do with the context of Hebrews, here are intriguing questions with no definitive answers![31]

Messengers, Watchers and Stewards[32]

From the references in chapter 13, it would seem that, for Hebrews, the leadership task is committed oversight, setting an example and giving faithful and authoritative guidance. Leaders are not endued with 'titles,' like elder, bishop or deacon. The word used to refer to them is, quite simply, a description of function: 'those who lead' (*hegoumenoi*). Here there is no suggestion of delineated hierarchy, of different 'orders' of leadership. And there is certainly no hint that these leaders are to be regarded as having special access to God. That would contradict one of Hebrews' major theological emphases. It is of no little significance that Hebrews does not describe 'those who lead' as priests. As he has made very clear in his sermon, this preacher sees the priesthood of Jesus as the priesthood to end all priesthoods. It is the expression of God's own priestliness. It can never be repeated, nor anywhere near effectively imitated. The only priest now needed to bring us to God is the one who lives for ever with God—Jesus. God's priestly life can be shared, certainly; but shared by everyone who looks to Jesus, not just a separated few. (Hebrews does not speak of Christians as 'a royal priesthood,' as does 1 Peter. Perhaps he wants to avoid that term, feeling it might lead to misunderstanding. But he would surely agree that Christ's priesthood is shared by all believers.[33]) Neither the old priesthood, nor a new form of specialist priesthood is

---
31 See Lane, Vol 1, pp lix–lx.
32 A phrase used of presbyters in Church of England ordination services (*BCP* and *ASB*).
33 Heb 3.14; 13.13,15,16.

required. Both would be superfluous—not to say misleading.

So, according to Hebrews, what is the role of church leaders? It is clear, first of all, that they are not to operate alone. In common with other New Testament writers, Hebrews speaks of a corporate leadership (all his references to leaders are plural). No individual has all the authority—nor all the responsibility. That is healthy. It guards against tyranny of various kinds, whether it be expressed in overwork, delusions of deity, abuse of power or the de-valuing of others. The only person in whom leadership can be absolutely and safely vested is God, the one who leads those who will follow into glory. To God alone the people of God owe their allegiance. And so do the people's leaders.

Following God's Lead

And God supremely, it seems, is given to leading in collaborative mode. Within God there is a perfect partnership of will and activity. The great work of creation, communication and salvation is shared with Son and Spirit (1.2–12; 2.2–4; 3.7; 7.25; 9.14; 10.12–17). Through Jesus the Son of God and Pioneer we see that God's leadership style involves taking bold initiatives, leading from the front (yet also from the middle and the edge) and refusing to give up, even when 'all hell breaks loose.' It means total commitment. It means holding on to a positive vision in the face of so much that would turn it into nightmare. It means extreme vulnerability—and the transforming triumph of love.

Only God can lead like this. But God also calls those who would follow his way to work with him, by and through his grace. Those who respond can expect to share something of God's costly ministry, even as they share the intimacy of God's love. God more than anyone perceives the potential of partnership—and is determined to realize it.

Some there will be whom God calls to express their 'collaboration' by serving the people of God through leading and guiding. Such human leaders are not to be despised but honoured and heeded. At 13.7, Hebrews bids his community 'remember' their past leaders, those who spoke the word of God to them. They are to learn from these worthies and imitate them, for they were messengers of God in what they proclaimed and in the way that they lived. Their preaching was backed up by exemplary and faithful lives. The fruit of such lives must be carefully looked at again and again. It should bring out a similar faithfulness in God's people.

Leaders, then, are those who communicate God's message in word and life; and in such a way as to call out faith in others. Verse 17 of chapter 13 gives us a further dimension. Leaders are those who keep watch over those entrusted to them, as people who will have to render account. The word used for keeping watch means, literally, going without sleep and staying alert (Mark 13.33; Luke 21.36; Ephesians 6.18). Those with oversight must be prepared to lose sleep over those for whom they are responsible! They also have to 'give an account'—that is, to God. They should be able to do this with joy rather than groaning. The latter is a strong word. It is used by Mark, for example, to describe the powerful spiritual and emotional activity going on within Jesus before he heals a deaf and dumb man (7.34). It is also used by Paul to describe the creation groaning in travail (Romans 8.22) and the groaning of this earthly body as it longs for its heavenly destiny (2 Corinthians 5.2). For leaders to render account with groaning would involve inner suffering at a deep level before God.

But such a state of affairs would not let the community off the hook. Leaders might be accountable but they are not vicariously responsible. If an unhappy account were to be rendered, that would be of 'no advantage' to the people. They, too, would have to face the consequences. Hebrews' sermon will have left them in no doubt of that. They must also obey and submit to those who lead them. Though such 'authority figures' are most certainly not God, they have been given (by a means Hebrews does not specify) the task of overseeing and guiding God's people. They must be respected and heeded.[34]

It may be that Hebrews' community had a particular problem in this area. Perhaps in the light of their less than wholehearted spiritual condition, leaders were for them an irksome pressure to whom they were inclined to pay little heed. It is interesting to speculate how the author himself may have fitted into the picture. He speaks with authority as one who expects to be heard. He is well-known to the community. He has an urgent concern for them. But he is clearly not one of their local leaders. Was he perhaps, like Paul, a travelling missionary, who had a special connection with this group of Christians? Whatever the truth of the matter, Hebrews is concerned that the group's leaders should receive that obedience which can move the community forward together.

According to Hebrews, those who lead have a crucial role in furthering the faithful pilgrimage of the people of God. They do so as fellow pilgrims.

---

[34] Interesting, here, to compare Ezekiel 33.1–9.

Bibliography

Commentaries on the English Text
F F Bruce, *The Epistle to the Hebrews* (London: Marshall, Morgan & Scott, 1965, rev 1990), (New London Commentaries). A modern 'classic'—very thorough and fair in its approach.
P Ellingworth, *The Epistle to the Hebrews* (London: Epworth, 1991). A very good 'starter.'
P E Hughes, *A Commentary on the Epistle to the Hebrews* (Grand Rapids: Eerdmans, 1977). Detailed, conservative evangelical approach which makes considerable use of patristic comment.
H W Montefiore, *A Commentary on the Epistle to the Hebrews* (London: Black's NT Commentaries, 1964). Takes as a working hypothesis that the Epistle was written by Apollos at Ephesus to the church at Corinth.
R McL Wilson, *Hebrews* (Grand Rapids: Eerdmans, 1987) (New Century Bible Commentary). A good, detailed exegesis.

Commentaries on the Greek Text
H W Attridge, *The Epistle to the Hebrews* (London: Hermeneia, 1989). A detailed and lively commentary, taking as its primary focus engagement with the text, rather than theories about the text.
P Ellingworth, *The Epistle to the Hebrews* (Grand Rapids: Eerdmans, 1993) (New International Greek Testament Commentary). An excellent commentary.
W L Lane, *Hebrews* (Waco: Word Biblical Commentary, 2 vols, 1991). Very good and very detailed. Definitely for those with 'prior learning'!
B F Westcott, *The Epistle to the Hebrews* (London: 1892) Produced towards the end of the 19th century, but still has many fascinating insights into Greek words and phrases.

Special Studies
B Lindars, *The Theology of the Letter to the Hebrews* (Cambridge, 1991). Easily accessible and thought-provoking.
L D Hurst, *The Epistle to the Hebrews: its background of thought* (Cambridge, 1990). A thorough discussion of possible influences on Hebrews which, refreshingly, ends with an engaging question.
J Dunnill, *Covenant and Sacrifice in the Letter to the Hebrews* (Cambridge, 1992). The working out of a structuralist interpretation.

See also comprehensive bibliography in Ellingworth's *Greek Testament Commentary*.